Meet the dinosaurs

Before you start reading *Argentinosaurus, Giant of Giants*, let's meet its main characters. Who are they? What do they look like? And where did they live?

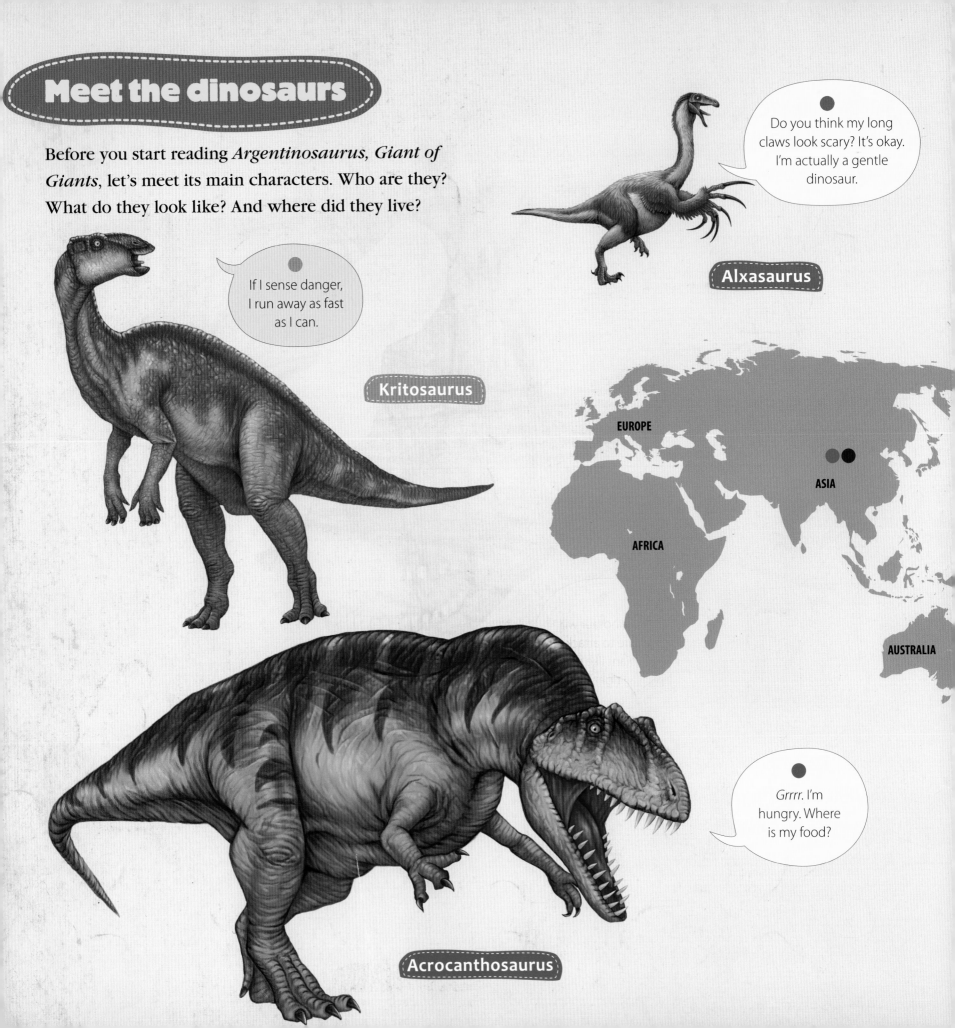

big & SMALL

Original Korean text and illustrations by Dreaming Tortoise
Korean edition © Aram Publishing

This English edition published by big & SMALL in 2016
by arrangement with Aram Publishing
English text edited by Scott Forbes
English edition © big & SMALL 2016

Distributed in the United States and Canada by
Lerner Publishing Group, Inc.
241 First Avenue North
Minneapolis, MN 55401 U.S.A.
www.lernerbooks.com

Photo credits:
Page 28, bottom: © saures
Page 29, bottom: © Giloun

ISBN: 978-1-925248-79-1
Printed in Korea

To learn about dinosaur fossils, see page 28.
For information on the main groups of dinosaurs,
see the Dinosaur Family Tree on page 30.

Argentinosaurus
Giant of Giants

Argentinosaurus

big & SMALL

Acrocanthosaurus

Two Acrocanthosaurus were out hunting. They hadn't eaten for a while and were starving. They saw a Sauropelta ahead of them. It looked like it would make a very tasty meal!

Acrocanthosaurus had curved claws at the ends of its fingers, which were perfect for holding on to large prey.

The two Acrocanthosaurus rushed toward the
Sauropelta. But when they saw the bony plates
on its back and the huge spikes on its shoulders
they stoppd in their tracks. Biting that could
be painful! So they moved off in search
of easier prey.

SAUROPELTA

GROUP: Ankylosaurs
DIET: Plants
WHEN IT LIVED: Early Cretaceous
WHERE IT LIVED: North America (USA)
LENGTH: 16.5–26 feet (5–8 meters)
HEIGHT: 6 feet (1.8 meters)
WEIGHT: 3 tons
(2.8 tonnes)

Soon the two Acrocanthosaurus spotted a Deinonychus
that had strayed away from its pack. They split up,
planning to attack the Deinonychus from two sides.
Then, at top speed, they charged down the hill
toward their prey.

Acrocanthosaurus wasn't as heavy as it appeared. It could run
fast – up to 25 miles per hour (40 kilometers per hour).

The name Acrocanthosaurus means "high-spined lizard." Acrocanthosaurus had a line of tall, thin bones that stuck up from its spine and supported its back muscles. Males had larger bumps than females and used them to attract mates.

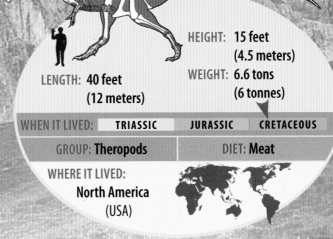

LENGTH: **40 feet** (12 meters)

HEIGHT: **15 feet** (4.5 meters)

WEIGHT: **6.6 tons** (6 tonnes)

WHEN IT LIVED: | **TRIASSIC** | **JURASSIC** | **CRETACEOUS**

GROUP: **Theropods**

DIET: **Meat**

WHERE IT LIVED: **North America** (USA)

DEINONYCHUS

GROUP: Theropods
DIET: Meat
WHEN IT LIVED: Early Cretaceous
WHERE IT LIVED: North America (USA)
LENGTH: 10–12 feet (3–3.5 meters)
HEIGHT: 4 feet (1.2 meters)
WEIGHT: 175–220 pounds (80–100 kilograms)

Kritosaurus

SAY IT:
Krit-oh-SAW-rus

Two Kritosaurus and
a Euoplocephalus were
munching on some tasty leaves.
They chomped and chewed for
hours, eating as much as they could.
They knew the dry season was coming.
Soon food would be hard to find.

Kritosaurus had a wide, flat mouth
that looked a bit like a duck's bill.
This broad bill was useful for grabbing branches
and pulling off leaves.
Inside its mouth were many rows of teeth.
These allowed it to chew and mash up
tough leaves and twigs.

EUOPLOCEPHALUS

GROUP: Ankylosaurs
DIET: Plants
WHEN IT LIVED: Late Cretaceous
WHERE IT LIVED: North America
(USA, Canada)
LENGTH: 16.5–20 feet (5–6 meters)
HEIGHT: 4–5 feet (1.2–1.5 meters)
WEIGHT: 2.2–4.4 tons
(2–4 tonnes)

When the dry season arrived, the dinosaurs
had to travel far and wide to find food.

As a group of Kritosaurus crossed the plains, a
Daspletosaurus appeared — a dangerous meat-eater.
The Kritosaurus turned and ran away at top speed.

For protection against meat-eating dinosaurs,
Kritosaurus often lived in large groups, or herds.

Fossils of Kritosaurus have been found over a wide area. This suggests that some Kritosaurus traveled long distances to find food. Some may even have journeyed between North America and South America.

DASPLETOSAURUS

GROUP: Theropods
DIET: Meat
WHEN IT LIVED: Late Cretaceous
WHERE IT LIVED: North America (Canada)
LENGTH: 30 feet (9 meters)
HEIGHT: 16.5 feet (5 meters)
WEIGHT: 2.2 tons (2 tonnes)

HEIGHT: 13 feet (4 meters)

LENGTH: 30 feet (9 meters)

WEIGHT: 3.3–5.5 tons (3–5 tonnes)

WHEN IT LIVED:	TRIASSIC	JURASSIC	CRETACEOUS

GROUP: Ornithopods	DIET: Plants

WHERE IT LIVED:
North America (USA, Canada), South America (Argentina)

Bambiraptor

A pack of Bambiraptors had spotted a young
Anatotitan that had strayed away from its group.
One Bambiraptor leaped onto the Anatotitan's back.
The others then swarmed
around their victim,
biting and ripping at its sides.

HEIGHT: 1.6 feet
(0.5 meters)

LENGTH: 3–4 feet
(1–1.3 meters)

WEIGHT: 7 pounds
(3 kilograms)

WHEN IT LIVED:	TRIASSIC	JURASSIC	CRETACEOUS
GROUP: Theropods		DIET: Meat	

WHERE IT LIVED:
North America
(USA)

Bambiraptor is named after the famous
Disney character, Bambi, the baby deer.
But Bambiraptor was anything but cute.
It was a sly and vicious hunter.
Its secret weapon was an extra-long,
extra-sharp curved claw on each foot.
It used this claw to slash and tear its prey.

ANATOTITAN

GROUP: Ornithopods
DIET: Plants
WHEN IT LIVED: Late Cretaceous
WHERE IT LIVED: North America
LENGTH: 30–40 feet (9–12 meters)
HEIGHT: 13–16.5 feet (4–5 meters)
WEIGHT: 3.3–4.4 tons
(3–6 tonnes)

Argentinosaurus

Boom … boom! The ground began to shake.
A herd of gigantic Argentinosaurus came
crashing out of the forest.

Argentinosaurus was one of the biggest dinosaurs ever.
But not even it was safe from fearsome meat-eaters.
A Giganotosaurus was preparing to attack!

A baby Argentinosaurus came out of an egg as small as a football.
It then took at least 15 years to grow to its full size.

A fully grown Argentinosaurus was as long as two school buses and as heavy as five. To supply energy for its enormous body, Argentinosaurus had to spend almost all day eating.

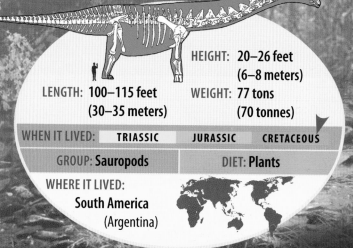

LENGTH: 100–115 feet
(30–35 meters)

HEIGHT: 20–26 feet
(6–8 meters)

WEIGHT: 77 tons
(70 tonnes)

WHEN IT LIVED:	TRIASSIC	JURASSIC	CRETACEOUS

GROUP: Sauropods	DIET: Plants

WHERE IT LIVED:
South America
(Argentina)

Another Giganotosaurus approached,
baring its long, pointed teeth.
The Argentinosaurus swung their
mighty tails at their attackers.
Whack! One Giganotosaurus
staggered back, injured.
The other turned and ran away.

GIGANOTOSAURUS

GROUP: Theropods
DIET: Meat
WHEN IT LIVED: Early Cretaceous
to late Cretaceous
WHERE IT LIVED: South America (Argentina)
LENGTH: 40–46 feet (12–14 meters)
HEIGHT: 23–26 feet (7–8 meters)
WEIGHT: 6.6–7.7 tons
(6–7 tonnes)

Alxasaurus

SAY IT:
Alk-sah-SAW-rus

The Alxasaurus saw a group of Microraptors approaching.
Alhough they were small, Microraptors could be fierce.
The Alxasaurus raised their long, curved claws,
ready to defend themselves.
At the sight of these huge claws,
the Microraptors ran away.

Alxasaurus did not normally use its claws
for hunting or fighting. Instead, it used them
to reach and grab plants, or to dig into
the ground to find insects.

MICRORAPTOR

GROUP: Theropods
DIET: Meat
WHEN IT LIVED: Early Cretaceous
WHERE IT LIVED: Asia (China, Korea)
LENGTH: 1.3–2.6 feet (40–80 centimeters)
HEIGHT: 1.3 feet (40 centimeters)
WEIGHT: 4.4–8.8 pounds
(2–4 kilograms)

The Alxasaurus watched the Microraptors run away. They had had a lucky escape. Attacking in a group, the small Microraptors could have killed them.

Once they were sure their enemies had gone, the Alxasaurus began feeding on some nearby trees.

Alxasaurus walked on two legs.
Because it had a long neck and
a short tail, it did not have good balance.
That meant it couldn't run very fast.

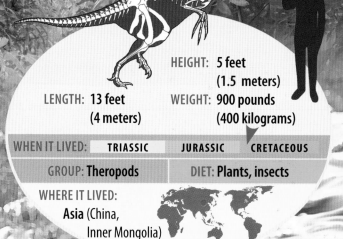

| HEIGHT: | 5 feet (1.5 meters) |
| LENGTH: 13 feet (4 meters) | WEIGHT: 900 pounds (400 kilograms) |

WHEN IT LIVED:	TRIASSIC	JURASSIC	CRETACEOUS
GROUP: **Theropods**		DIET: **Plants, insects**	

WHERE IT LIVED:
Asia (China, Inner Mongolia)

23

Huayangosaurus

SAY IT:
Why-yang-go-SAW-rus

The Dilophosaurus knew that Huayangosaurus was a slow-moving dinosaur. It moved in quietly, hoping to surprise its prey. The Huayangosaurus looked up just in time.

Huayangosaurus had pointy plates all along its back. These made it look bigger and fiercer than it really was, and helped scare off attackers.

DILOPHOSAURUS

GROUP: Theropods
DIET: Meat
WHEN IT LIVED: Early Jurassic
WHERE IT LIVED: North America (USA),
Asia (China)
LENGTH: 16.5–20 feet (5–6 meters)
HEIGHT: 6 feet (1.8 meters)
WEIGHT: 0.55 tons
(0.5 tonnes)

Thwack! The Huayangosaurus struck the Dilophosaurus with its spiky tail. The Dilophosaurus limped off in pain. It hadn't realized that Huayangosaurus could defend itself so well. From now on, it would steer clear of this spiky plant-eater.

LENGTH: 15 feet
(4.5 meters)

HEIGHT: 5 feet
(1.5 meters)

WEIGHT: 1–1.1 tons
(0.9–1 tonnes)

WHEN IT LIVED:	TRIASSIC	JURASSIC	CRETACEOUS

GROUP: Stegosaurs	DIET: Plants

WHERE IT LIVED:
Asia (China)

Huayangosaurus was similar to the famous
dinosaur Stegosaurus, but quite a lot smaller.
Like Stegosaurus, it may have used the plates
on its back to attract a mate.

Dinosaur Fossils

Fossils are the remains of dinosaurs. They can be hard parts of dinosaurs, such as bones and teeth, that have slowly turned to stone. Or they may be impressions of bones, teeth, or skin preserved in rocks.

▲ Model of Acrocanthosaurus skeleton

Acrocanthosaurus

Fossils of Acrocanathosaurus were first found in Oklahoma, USA, in 1956. After studying these, scientists gave the dinosaur its name. Since that time, many other Acrocanthosaurus fossils have been found, including a complete skeleton in 1990 and many fossilized teeth. Scientists have also found fossilized footprints, including some made by a group of Acrocanthosaurus as they were chasing other dinosaurs.

Kritosaurus

The first Kritosaurus fossil was found by Doctor Barnum Brown, a famous US dinosaur hunter, in 1910, in southern New Mexico, USA. Before that, fossils of similar duck-billed dinosaurs, such as Hadrosaurus, had been found all over northern North America. The Kritosaurus fossil was the first one to be uncovered in the southern part of North America.

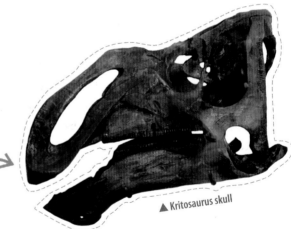

▲ Kritosaurus skull

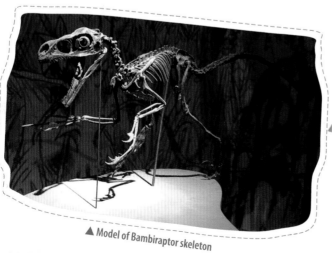

▲ Model of Bambiraptor skeleton

Bambiraptor

It was a 14-year-old boy, Wes Linster, who first discovered a fossil of Bambiraptor. He was out looking for dinosaur bones with his parents in 1993, in Montana, USA. The fossil was a complete skeleton of a young Bambiraptor, almost perfectly preserved. "Bambi" was the name of the main character in the Disney animated film of the same name, a young deer. Fossils of adult Bambiraptors have since been found.

▶ Model of Argentinosaurus skeleton

Argentinosaurus

A farmer living in Argentina came across the first Argentinosaurus fossil, in 1987. At first, he thought the fossilized bone was a large chunk of wood.
So far, no one has found a complete Argentinosaurus skeleton. But by studying fossils of the dinosaur's legs and backbones, scientists have worked out how large it was and created life-size model skeletons.

Alxasaurus

Like its relatives Therizinosaurus and Beipiaosaurus, Alxasaurus had extremely long, blade-like claws. The first Alxasaurus fossil was found in the Alxa Desert of Inner Mongolia, China. The dinosaur was named in 1993 by Canadian scientist Dale Russell and Chinese dinosaur hunter Dong Zhiming.

▲ Model of Alxasaurus skeleton

▶ Model of Huayangosaurus skeleton

Huayangosaurus

The first fossil of Huayangosaurus was found in 1979 in Tzekung, in China's Sichuan province. The dinosaur is named for the old name for the region of Sichuan, "Huayang". It was named by Chinese dinosaur hunter Dong Zhiming in 1982.

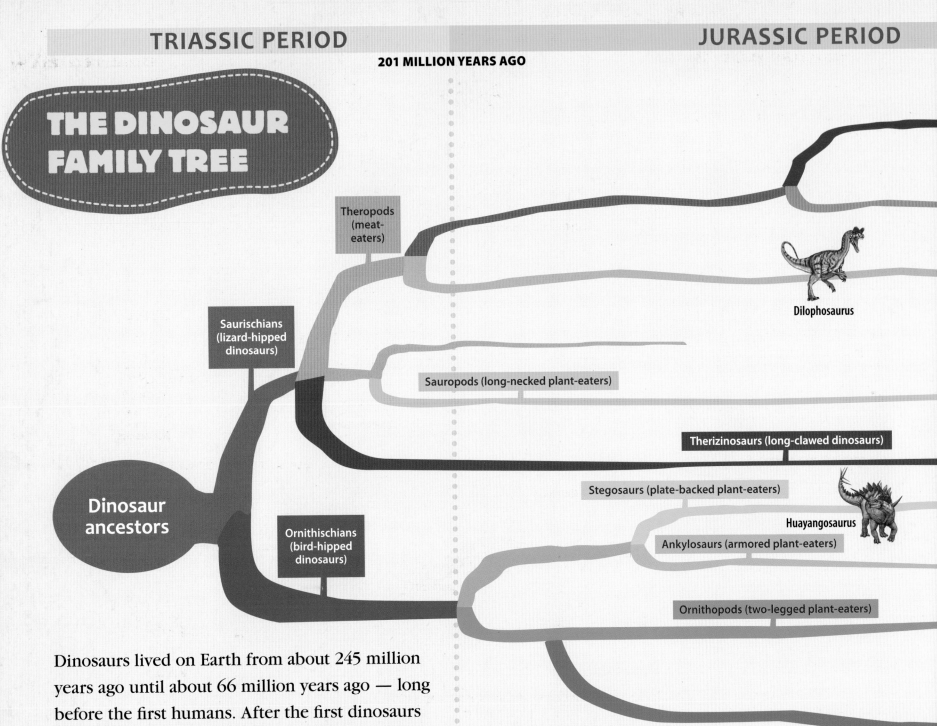

THE DINOSAUR FAMILY TREE

Theropods (meat-eaters)

Dilophosaurus

Saurischians (lizard-hipped dinosaurs)

Sauropods (long-necked plant-eaters)

Therizinosaurs (long-clawed dinosaurs)

Stegosaurs (plate-backed plant-eaters)

Huayangosaurus

Dinosaur ancestors

Ornithischians (bird-hipped dinosaurs)

Ankylosaurs (armored plant-eaters)

Ornithopods (two-legged plant-eaters)

Dinosaurs lived on Earth from about 245 million years ago until about 66 million years ago — long before the first humans. After the first dinosaurs appeared, they spread to all the continents and many different kinds of dinosaurs emerged. This chart shows the main groups of dinosaurs.

Pterosaurs (flying reptiles)

Ichthyosaurs (marine reptiles)

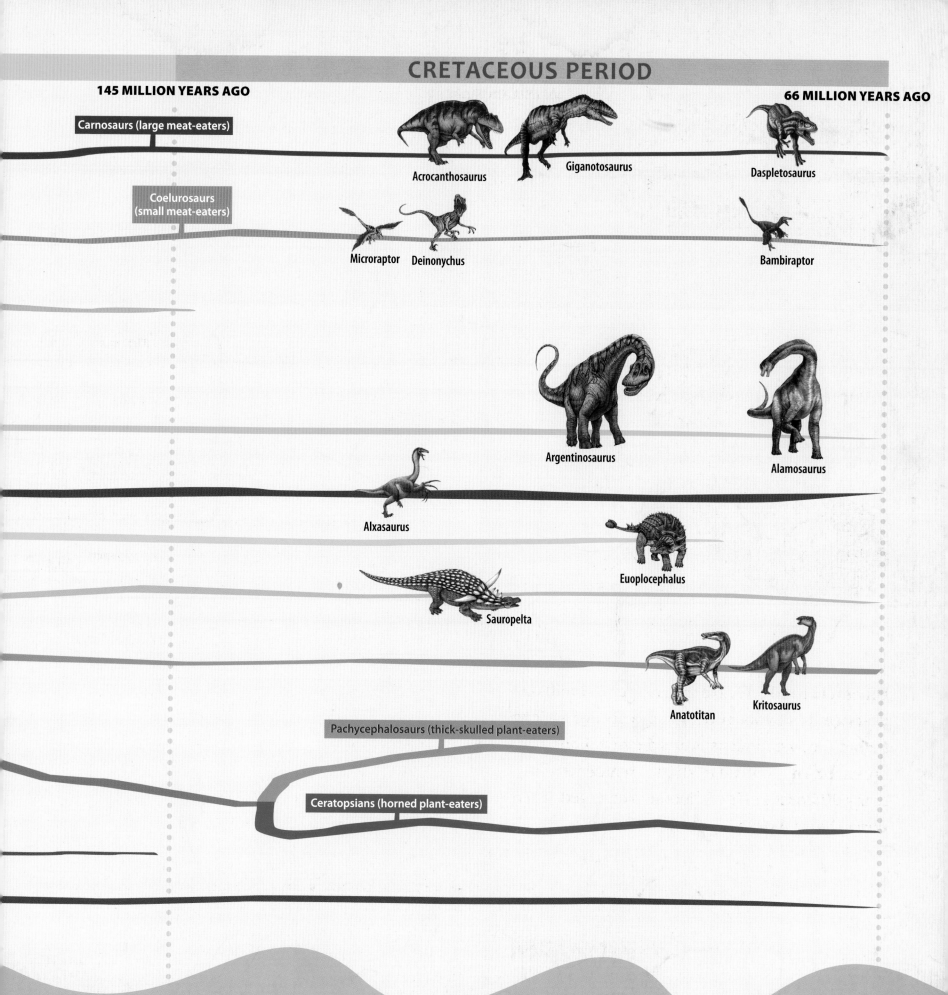

CRETACEOUS PERIOD

145 MILLION YEARS AGO

66 MILLION YEARS AGO

Carnosaurs (large meat-eaters)

Acrocanthosaurus

Giganotosaurus

Daspletosaurus

Coelurosaurs (small meat-eaters)

Microraptor

Deinonychus

Bambiraptor

Argentinosaurus

Alamosaurus

Alxasaurus

Euoplocephalus

Sauropelta

Anatotitan

Kritosaurus

Pachycephalosaurs (thick-skulled plant-eaters)

Ceratopsians (horned plant-eaters)